CRAFTS

OF THE MIDDLE AGES™

THE CRAFTS AND CULTURE OF A
MEDIEVAL GUILD

Joann Jovinelly and Jason Netelkos

The Rosen Publishing Group, Inc., New York

For Mom, a spirited and creative woman who taught me it was possible to make magic

Published in 2007 by The Rosen Publishing Group, Inc.
29 East 21st Street, New York, NY 10010

Library of Congress Cataloging-in-Publication Data

Jovinelly, Joann.
The crafts and culture of a medieval guild/Joann Jovinelly and Jason Netelkos.—1st ed.
   p. cm.—(Crafts of the Middle Ages)
Includes bibliographical references and index.
Summary: Includes instructions for making jewelry, stone carving designs, a peasant's hat, shoes, armor, pottery, etc. from available materials.
ISBN 1-4042-0757-0 (library binding)
1. Guilds—Europe—History—Juvenile literature. 2. Artisans—Europe—History—Juvenile literature. 3. Europe—Commerce—History—To 1500—Juvenile literature. 4. Middle Ages—Juvenile literature. 5. Handicraft—Juvenile literature. I. Title. II. Series: Jovinelly, Joann. Crafts of the Middle Ages.
HD6456.J68 2007
338.6'320940902—dc22

2005035899

Manufactured in the United States of America

Note to Parents
Some of these projects require tools or materials that can be dangerous if used improperly. Adult supervision will be necessary when projects require the use of a craft knife, cut aluminum, an oven, plaster of paris, or pins and needles. Before starting any of the projects in this book, you may want to cover your work area with newspaper or plastic. In addition, we recommend using a piece of thick cardboard to protect surfaces while cutting with craft or mat knives. We encourage you to discuss safety with your children and note in advance which projects may require your supervision.

CONTENTS

MEDIEVAL CULTURE

The guilds of the Middle Ages were associations of like-minded people who regulated a particular industry, such as masonry or weaving. They were much like today's labor unions. The idea of guilds originated during ancient times, and a few associations from the Roman era continued to thrive during the Medieval period. Historians refer to the 1,000-year span between the ancient Roman Empire and the fifteenth-century Renaissance as the Middle Ages.

Medieval guilds were highly organized societies, often linked by their common industry and system of beliefs. In this painting, Flemish artist Denis van Alsloot depicts a procession of Dutch guild masters in 1616.

Guilds were important during the Middle Ages when towns were developing. In order to protect their assets and increase their profits, guild members became active in local government, eventually helping towns gain political independence from reigning lords. They helped establish businesses and ushered in a period of economic stability and relative peace in western Europe.

After the migrations of various Germanic, Slavic, and Asiatic groups in the fourth and fifth centuries, and the Viking raids of the eighth century, western Europe had stabilized by AD 1000. Conflicts no longer took up the majority of people's attention, the population increased, and agricultural

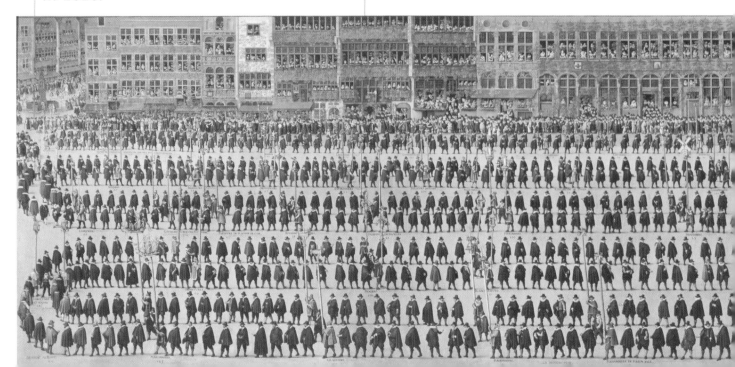

This map of medieval Europe depicts the land and sea shipping routes of major trading companies of the period. Business centers and maritime trade routes were consistently developing during the Middle Ages.

advancements allowed for increased food production. People were no longer interested in obtaining goods only for survival. They wanted luxury items such as pottery, carpets, tapestries, fur-

niture, and jewelry. The merchant economy was taking shape, and regional and overseas trade increased.

As the development of guilds followed, western Europe was transformed. The medieval economy was originally based upon feudalism (a social and economic system based on land ownership, power distribution, and farming). After the development of guilds, it changed into an economy based on the production of goods, consumerism, and trade.

Entire towns sometimes formed alliances to protect their trading interests. One of the most famous examples of such an alliance took place to protect trade around the Baltic Sea. These guilds were called the Hanseatic League—from the German word *hanse*, meaning "association." Member towns throughout northern Germany became known as Hanse towns. Guild members established trading centers, controlled piracy, built lighthouses, and improved navigation in order to increase trade and protect traveling merchants. The Hanseatic League reached its zenith during the fourteenth century by dominating trade with Russian and Scandinavian kingdoms. It played a key role in advancing trade and the exchange of ideas throughout northern Europe.

THE FIRST GUILDS

The only guilds that evolved past the ancient period were a few organizations of glassmakers and stonecutters. Members of these guilds—or gilds, a term that originally indicated their wealth in gold deposits—were initially unwelcome members of medieval society, especially by the Catholic Church. Because of their sworn oaths to uphold loyalty to their brethren no matter the circumstances, the morality of guild members was considered questionable.

After AD 1000, as the population of western Europe increased, agricultural techniques improved. Fewer people were needed to work the land, and towns were established. Merchants and artisans were the "landless people" who helped build towns. However, they were two distinctly different groups during the Middle Ages. Anyone who made goods was considered a craftsman or an artisan. Merchants and traders earned money by selling the goods of others. Certain craftsmen did sell their own finished wares, but they did not consider themselves merchants.

Medieval merchants were the first to form guilds in western Europe, doing so around the twelfth century. Soon, every town had a merchant guild. Craftsmen then formed guilds in

A cloth merchant displays his fabrics in this fourteenth-century manuscript illumination. Before craft guilds were formed and business areas were established, vendors traveled from town to town to sell their goods.

response to the creation of the merchant guilds. Craft guilds became widespread by the thirteenth century.

There was often fighting between the two groups, and craftsmen wanted to guard against the privileges they saw merchants taking for themselves. Craftsmen became concerned with the need to control the design and quality of their work. They also wanted control over the supply and demand of the goods they produced. To accomplish these goals, they decided to set standards of quality and workmanship. They wished to protect their trade, and they wanted control over how many people learned their profession and what price could be charged for their goods.

Bakers, tailors, stonecutters, painters, tanners, and butchers each had their own guild. Even occupations that would not immediately come to mind formed guild associations. According to a list of Florentine businesses subject to tax in 1316, wine merchants, mattress makers, dice makers, money changers, and makers of hats and caps were all subject to a guild-related tax.

Each craft guild supported its members and their families. Once fully established, membership was limited. It was in this way that the guild ensured a decent level of earnings for its members. This stability was just one of the benefits of membership. Besides a steady income, guild members had security. Should one member die, the other members of the guild took in the deceased person's family, helped educate his children, paid his widow for the funeral expenses, and, at times, fed his family.

Both merchant and craft guilds were important for different reasons. Merchant guilds influenced a departure from the feudal system, urging kings and lords to allow guilds to set the laws regarding manufacturing and trade. Craft guilds helped support individual workers by creating monopolies over the production of most goods. Their continuous business remained stable since outside merchants were not allowed to intervene.

POWERFUL FRATERNITIES

Like labor unions do today, medieval merchant and craft guilds set and regulated the standards by which their members worked. The guilds set hours, controlled the quality of the goods produced, the amount of money a member could earn, and who could be admitted into the guild.

Guilds were mostly formed to discourage competition. If, for instance, another merchant or trader wanted to sell his wares for a lesser price, he was ordered not to do so. The same held true if he wanted to manufacture his goods using updated technology, such as with the use of a waterwheel to speed production. Unless all guild members had use of the same technology, it was forbidden. By the same token, no employer could request that his artisans work longer hours, use better supplies or ingredients, or pay higher wages. Guilds were not permitted to lure artisans from other shops.

Merchant and craft guilds had strong associations with the church as well. Many had patron saints (holy spirits honored as guardians or protectors). Saint John was the patron saint of the stonemasons, for instance. Saint Martin was the patron saint of the fullers (workmen who cleaned and thickened freshly woven cloth), and Saint Joseph was the patron saint of carpentry. Members often gathered for lavish celebrations on their saints' feast days and to choose leaders. Guilds gave regularly to church charities and participated in church functions. It was also common for town charters to include in their guild rules that members make regular payments to the church on holy days such as Christmas. At the same time, it was very often the guild members who put on Passion plays to celebrate the life of Jesus Christ during Easter week.

This oil painting by Petrus Christus features a goldsmith in his shop with a young couple shopping for a wedding ring. It was commissioned by the goldsmiths guild of Bruges in 1449. The main figure may also be a likeness of Saint Eligius, the patron saint of goldsmiths.

FROM APPRENTICE TO MASTER

Master craftsmen were the top artisans in their field, and they passed on the secrets of their craft to younger apprentices. Masters owned the shops where they worked and usually lived in the upper levels with their family. In many instances, they rented out half of their shops to other craftsmen.

Masters generally took in one or two apprentices, for whom they provided shelter, clothing, and food. Usually, these apprentices were teenage boys between the ages of eleven and fourteen. Teenage girls also became apprentices, though they were normally taught by a craftsman's wife.

Apprentices usually specialized in a certain field because of their family connections. Wealthier families were offered the best apprenticeships. In some cases, a child could apprentice with his or her father, but this was unlikely. Widows also continued the work of their deceased husbands, especially if their craft involved brewing, weaving, sewing, dyeing, or making cloth.

In most instances, parents paid a fee to the master to allow their son or daughter to be taught by him. It took between two and twelve years of careful study by an apprentice to learn his or her master's craft. During this period, male apprentices were never allowed to take a wife.

Teenage apprentices worked from sunrise to sunset and lived without luxury, often in the attic of the master's shop. They shared meals with the master's family and often helped with chores. While under the care of a master, apprentices were supposed to get an education and learn decent moral behavior.

Apprentices shared space with a journeyman, an older teenager who had learned his craft well enough to earn a salary. After a period of two to seven years, apprentices rose to the level of journeyman. A journeyman could also travel, taking with him a letter from his master stating that he could learn skills related to his craft from other masters. It is in this way that the various techniques of the craft trades were shared throughout Europe.

Unlike the apprentice, who was permitted to use tools provided by his master, a journeyman had to provide his own tools and materials. Eventually, the guild's members rated a journeyman according to his talent. This test was usually based upon a journeyman's masterpiece, a project that sometimes took years to complete since he was permitted to pursue personal work only on Sundays. Some journeymen never became master craftsmen. Either they ran out of money and could not finish their masterpiece or they were never admitted to their guild. This lack of admission often occurred if the economy in the town was poor. Guild members purposely kept journeymen from becoming masters in order to control the amount of people who could provide a particular good or service in any town.

In this French miniature painting, a mason and a carpenter work under a master craftsman (center). *Children often started their apprenticeships early, many beginning from the age of seven years, so that by adulthood all were highly skilled in their craft.*

SUCCESSES AND CONFLICTS

In many places, guilds were so successful that few trades were practiced without a guild. In some cases, even thieves and beggars formed guildlike associations.

Occasionally, however, trouble within the guilds erupted. Such was the case in thirteenth-century England when officers of the cloth-workers guild excluded some members. These excluded people, called fullers or dyers, were the artisans who stained their hands while working the cloth. Guild members called them "blue-nails" for the stains on their hands. In retaliation, the fullers and dyers formed their own guilds. Over time, many different craftsmen that made up the English fabric industry also formed independent associations.

As previously mentioned, German Hanse towns were among the most successful guilds. They had tremendous control over all of the trade in northern Europe. In part, the strength and power of the Hanseatic League emerged out of self-defense. Fledgling towns along the North and Baltic Seas were under constant threat from Viking warriors during the early Middle Ages. It was only after banding together that these towns established safe and profitable land and sea trade routes. One of the league's strengths was the idea of a commercial boycott, or *verhansung*, of its enemies. An organized boycott—when people and companies willfully did not buy a trader's goods—was an effective means of weakening its business. The league also gained strength because it helped establish a common currency.

Guilds remained powerful into the Renaissance, the fifteenth-century period of rebirth that followed the

Guild meetings like this one depicting the guild of fish sellers in a fourteenth-century Italian painting took place frequently. Guild members took part in making decisions and gathered for personal as well as professional occasions.

Middle Ages. Although many of the guilds and their customs and traditions transitioned seamlessly into the Renaissance, many of the guilds in northern Europe weakened or broke apart entirely. By 1630, most of the powerful Hanseatic League had disbanded.

More conflicts between townspeople erupted as some guilds gained a tremendous amount of wealth and power. There was a growing resentment among the lower classes toward the consolidation of power among influential master craftsmen. By the end of the Middle Ages, guild masters had so much power that they began to oversee the guilds' production as a means to earn their own inflated incomes. Many

started buying raw materials and selling the goods to the craftsmen for a profit. Some even earned money by buying and reselling finished products.

Soon, craftsmen resented these guild masters and their exploitation methods. The power of the guilds started to ebb away.

Throughout the Middle Ages, however, guilds had protected workers and inspired and regulated trade. They had helped western Europe grow from a feudal economy to one based on the production and sale of goods and services. Finally, guilds helped people break away from feudal ties to lords and kings to form their own towns and establish the right to govern themselves.

Life in a Medieval Guild

Many guilds had their own guildhall where they met to discuss regulations, settle fines, and make decisions about whether or not journeymen applying for membership could be admitted. Usually, these meetings ended with a serving of homemade ale (beer).

Guildhalls were lavishly decorated. They had painted interiors and wooden beams (often in geometric patterns), and they sometimes featured a painted coat of arms. Guildhalls stored members' supplies and were also used for celebratory events, such as banquets that were held on the anniversary of the guild's patron saint. When not being used for meetings and feasts, guildhalls were occasionally a place for townspeople to attend holiday performances, such as Passion plays. If such a guildhall did not exist, members met at the local church, where they often had their own altars, chaplains, and chapels.

Guild members regularly cleaned the town's streets, removed garbage, kept watch during the night, and provided food for those who were hungry. Sometimes they helped construct buildings or walls to defend the town. They considered these acts their civic

Members of the Guild of Cutlers—medieval craftsmen who made, repaired, and sold knives and swords—built this guildhall in Essex, England, in 1390. It has since been used as a grammar school and is today a community center.

responsibility and could compete with other guilds for prestige in this way. More than anything, however, guilds provided for the well-being of their members and their families. They sponsored funerals for deceased members and provided dowries for members' female children who were to be married. Some guilds even provided members a form of health insurance and contributed to the education of their children.

Both merchant and craft guilds had their own individual laws and practices, and notices from every guild were distinctive because each one had its own seal. Because guild activities were both secular and religious, these seals usually contained a variety of symbolic imagery, including a guild's patron saint and the tools of its craft. A great deal of pride was associated with guild membership and of being accepted into the guild as a master craftsman.

In this fourteenth-century manuscript illumination, a representative of Venice's weavers' guild offers a book of its statutes to Francesco Foscari, the doge of Venice from 1423 to 1457. Guild statutes regulated who could join a guild and set entrance fees for their inclusion.

This merchant guild seal dates from about 1300. During the Middle Ages, merchant guilds regulated trade between kingdoms, while individual craft guilds controlled the quality, appearance, price, and production of goods.

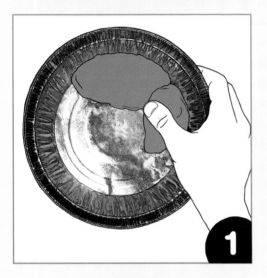

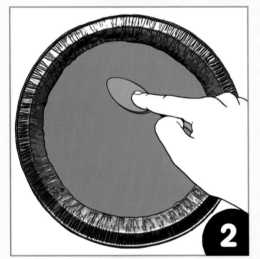

Guild Seal

Create a merchant guild seal. You can copy this one from 1300, or you can make an original design.

YOU WILL NEED

- Round aluminum pie plate
- Modeling clay
- Metal teaspoon
- Small bowl
- Ballpoint pen
- Toothpicks
- Plaster of paris
- Large paper clip
- Craft paint/brushes
- Cotton swabs
- Rubber gloves/smock

Step 1

To make this merchant seal, begin by making a mold. Fill the bottom of your aluminum pie plate with 1/2 inch of modeling clay. Take small amounts of clay and press it into the bottom of your pie plate, creating an even layer.

Step 2

Smooth the surface of the clay with the flat side of a metal spoon, as shown.

Step 3

Press the rim of a small bowl in the center of your modeling clay to make an impression of a circle. Inside this circle is where you will draw your merchant seal design.

Step 4

Make another circle in the clay with a ballpoint pen or toothpick, about 1/2 inch from the edge of the first circle. Fill this space with your name or the name of your merchant guild. Since your seal will be molded from this clay, the letters you write must be written backwards. You can personalize your seal by pressing small objects into the clay to make impressions, such as key chains, figurines, or toys, or you can draw on it with a

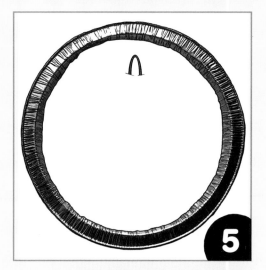

ballpoint pen or toothpick. Simple lines and textured bricks were used to create the fortified gate in this seal.

Step 5

When you are finished drawing your design into the clay, mix your plaster according to the package instructions. Wear rubber gloves and a smock to protect your hands and clothes. Fill the mold with plaster. Act fast before the plaster has time to set. Have a large paperclip ready to set into the wet plaster to hang your seal.

Step 6

When dry, remove from the foil pie plate. Flip over your seal and allow time to dry on the reverse side. Once dry, paint with layers of watered-down craft paint and remove excess pigment with a wet cotton swab. Use care to control the amount of water you use! You don't want to weaken the plaster.

Goldsmiths

oldsmiths recycled gold from older works of art, jewelry, and other acquired items. The gold was melted down in a smelting pot and applied over other metals to make jewelry. Goldsmiths also made gold leaf, the paper-thin sheets of gold that were used to decorate medieval manuscripts. To make repairs, goldsmiths made thin gold coils that could be heated to reattach stones or resize items.

Goldsmiths were among the medieval world's finest craftsmen. Besides working with gold, they made elaborate enamel inlays and cut and mounted precious gemstones. The goldsmith spent about half his time working with silver and was often commissioned by the church to make official items for Mass, such as candlesticks, alter cruets (containers for holding wine), enameled bowls and chalices, and incense burners.

Goldsmiths were skilled jewelry makers, and they produced a variety of popular items, such as brooches, belt buckles, earrings, and pendants.

This colored woodcut, which depicts the interior of a jeweler's shop, is from Hortus Sanitatis (The Origin of Health), *a medieval manuscript of herbal remedies. It was featured in an edition from 1491.*

Rings were extremely popular and were worn on all fingers including the thumb. Some were designed with the belief that they could cure diseases and guard the wearer against certain dangers, such as being poisoned. Others were set with stones that were meant to calm those who wore them, while some were inscribed with prayers or sentiments of love. A few of these love rings, usually shaped with clasped hands, were called posy rings, after the French word *poésie*, meaning poetry. Anyone engaged in business transactions often wore initial rings that they would use to press into wax seals when corresponding with business partners and associates.

Most goldsmiths stored gold and silver in strong chests for safekeeping. Sometimes they also stored valuable items for others. In time, some goldsmiths became moneylenders. Because they often had more money than other craftsmen, goldsmiths formed powerful guilds. In London, one of the members of the goldsmiths' guild became mayor of the city. Italian goldsmiths were just as wealthy and powerful. By the late Middle Ages, most Florentine goldsmiths had their shops on the Ponte Vecchio, the bridge over the Arno River where craftsmen's shops were grouped together. Similarly, the goldsmiths of Paris grouped their shops over the Seine River.

This medieval earring dates back to the sixth century. Goldsmiths were highly skilled at setting precious stones, creating enamel inlays, and working in ornate detail. Jewelry of all types remained popular throughout the Middle Ages.

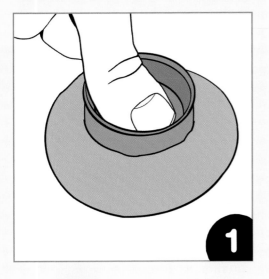

1

Jewelry*

Try your hand at being a master goldsmith by making medieval jewelry.

* ADULT SUPERVISION IS ADVISED FOR THIS CRAFT.

YOU WILL NEED

- **Oven-bake clay**
- **Small round objects:** plastic bottle caps, glue stick cap, and pens
- **Toothpicks**
- **Scissors**
- **Safety pins**
- **Craft paint/brushes**
- **Gloss medium**

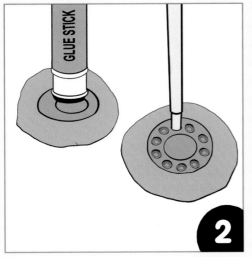

2

Step 1
Take a palm-sized ball of clay and flatten it into a disc. Press the back of a large bottle cap into the clay to make a round impression, as shown. This will become your mold. If you want to make more than one design, create several molds.

Step 2
Use the cap of a glue stick to make a smaller circular impression in the center of the first one. Use the bottom of a ballpoint pen to make even smaller designs within the first two circles.

Step 3
Next, make lines to separate the design into sections with toothpicks. Make the lines deep into the clay. Trace the outer circle with a deep line. When your design is complete, bake the clay according to the instructions on the package.

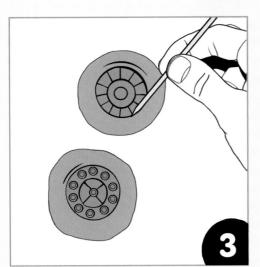

3

Step 4
After your clay mold has cooled, take small balls of clay and press them into the mold to make positive impressions, as shown. Remove them from the mold and cut off the excess clay with scissors. Smooth the edges with your fingers.

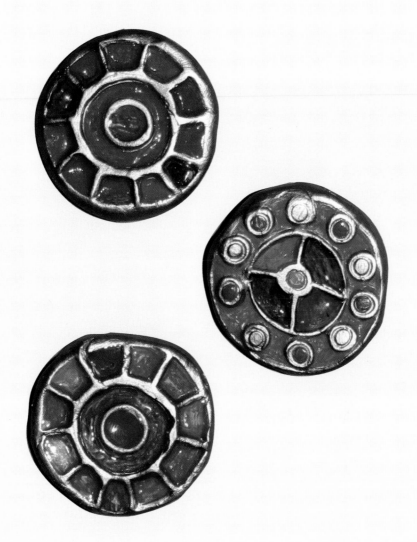

Step 5

Turn the piece over onto a flat, smooth surface and gently press a safety pin into the reverse side. Roll a tiny ball of clay and press it over the interior edge of the safety pin to hold it in place, as shown. Bake the jewelry pieces, safety pins included.

Step 6

After the jewelry pieces have baked and cooled, paint them bright colors. After the paint has dried, drip gloss medium into the spaces, as shown. When it dries it will make the jewelry appear as if it's been enameled.

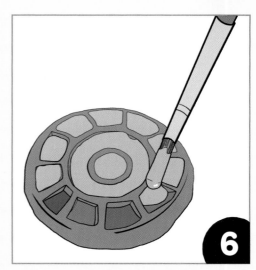

Stonemasons

This detail of a marble relief by Florentine sculptor Nanni di Banco shows medieval stonemasons and carpenters at work. Both stonemasons and carpenters were members of Florence's Arte di Pietra e Legname, or the Guild of Stone and Woodworkers.

Stonemasons, the men whose job it was to erect the stone cathedrals and castles of the Middle Ages, were among the first craftsmen to organize a guild. They were also among those who joined a variety of different guilds during their lifetime, picking up their tools and traveling to locations where work was available. Unlike most other tradesmen, stonemasons were used to working in groups, not in isolation. In addition, the guilds had little regulation over a stonemason's salary, which was unique among those trades that formed guilds.

Building cathedrals and other large stone structures required the skills of a variety of workers, not all of them guild members. General laborers, the men responsible for transporting stone and carrying plaster, were nonmembers at the bottom of the scale who were paid by the day. Stonemasons, intent on protecting who would and wouldn't be admitted into the guild, generally looked down upon day laborers and hired as few as possible. Morris Bishop's *The Middle Ages* recalls the plight of a man whose piety brought him to serve the stonemasons for pennies a day. The masons, who wanted nothing more than to protect their rights and salaries, killed him in cold blood.

The architect-engineer on most projects was also the guild master, or the head of the guild. He was responsible for recruiting all the workers and overseeing labor costs. Usually his contract was lavish and lasted several years. The architect-engineer established a stonemason's lodge on the site where meetings were held, meals were eaten, and secrets of the trade were discussed. The lodge also functioned as a storage facility for tools, ladders, wood, and other materials. The architect-engineer also helped provide housing for many of his masons who lived on or near the project site.

According to historian Jean Gimpel, author of *The Cathedral Builders*, there was a clear hierarchy of jobs related to the field of masonry. Porters, cementers, mortarmen, and stonecutters were considered equal, while plasterers, plaster mixers, and masons comprised a secondary group. For the most part, all of the work ceased during the winter months, so many stonemasons were also skilled at a second trade. Others traveled to warmer climates where work was continuous.

In order to section lines into equal segments, medieval masons used dividers like this one, a two-pronged tool like a mathematical compass. Medieval masons used repeated geometric proportions to build cathedrals, ratios they believed were divinely inspired. Often they incorrectly assumed that these proportions would protect the cathedrals from collapse.

The gargoyle in this photograph is a part of the Cathedral of Notre Dame in Paris, France. It rests high above the Parisian streets on top of the cathedral, which was finished in 1250.

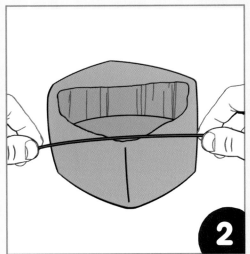

Gargoyle

Pretend that you are a master stone carver. You have been commissioned to create a gargoyle for the Cathedral of Notre Dame in Paris, France.

YOU WILL NEED

- 5 lb. box of ceramic or terra-cotta clay
- Clay carving tools or utensils, such as spoons and forks
- Sponge
- Small bowl for making "slip"
- Flexible wire
- Old towels/plastic bag
- Newspaper

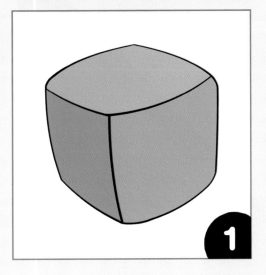

Step 1

Remove all the clay from the box and knead it for roughly ten minutes to remove air bubbles. Kneading also makes the clay pliable. Next, form the clay into a square block. Fill a small bowl with cold water. Add to the water a small amount of clay, roughly a quarter of a teaspoon. This clay, once diluted, will make "slip," a bonding agent that should be used when adding additional clay to your sculpture.

Step 2

To make your gargoyle, remove sections of the clay with wire. Try to visualize the gargoyle inside the block. The first cut you make with the wire will be the bridge of the nose. To do this, remove the corner facing you with wire at a 90-degree angle.

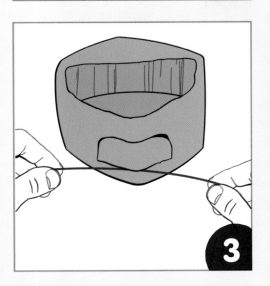

Step 3

The second cut will help you position where the snout ends and the mouth begins, as shown. Using both hands, guide the wire in a smooth motion to slice the clay.

Step 4

Next, use your fingers to pull the clay up on both sides, extending corners into spiked ears and inserting

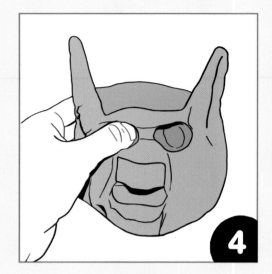

your fingers into the clay to make eye sockets. Use your fingers to hollow the gargoyle's mouth.

Step 5

By now you should have a small pile of excess clay. You'll need this clay to build up areas as you sculpt. For instance, you'll want to add a sphere to the inside of the eye sockets, lips along the mouth, and detail to the nose. To help you carve your clay, use standard clay tools or cooking utensils. Forks can create texture; spoons can help hollow the clay; and sponges and spatulas can help smooth it.

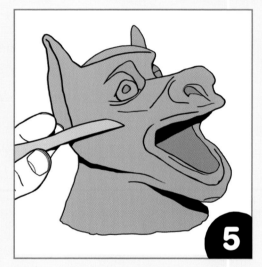

Step 6

If you want to finish your sculpture later, wrap it in dampened paper towels and cover it with a plastic bag. To dry your sculpture completely, allow the air to hit it directly. Some clays can be air-dried and others are baked in a standard oven or fired in a kiln. Follow the specific directions for drying on your package of clay.

Bakers

T he bakers' guild was among the most regulated of all the medieval guilds. The first bakers' guild on record was located in Pontoise, France, where King Louis VII allowed bakers to organize in 1162. In addition to the guild's supervision over a baker's salary, the weight and price of each loaf of bread was controlled, as well as the type of flour used to bake it. (Weights changed from year to year depending on the availability of grain.)

Individual loaves were identified by a baker's mark, which was pressed into the underside of the bread. Bakers who cheated customers by offering uneven weights of loaves, stale bread, or bread made from poor ingredients were sent into the town square where they were publicly humiliated. Considering the evidence recorded in medieval court records, regulations were necessary. People sometimes reported bread made with sand or dirt instead of flour. Some customers even became feverish and delirious, having been afflicted with ergotism, a disease

This lively scene of traveling bakers is part of a fifteenth-century German manuscript, A Chronicle of the Council of Constance, *by Ulrich von Richental. It is a rich diary of Richental's experiences and is now prized for its variety of illustrations of daily life during the Middle Ages.*

caused by eating bread made from moldy grain. Bakers found guilty of using spoiled ingredients were usually locked in a pillory (a wooden frame with holes for the head and hands) with one of their substandard loaves hanging around their neck.

A baker's life was difficult. In times of famine or grain shortages, he was often subject to changing laws that forced him to lower his prices even though the cost of grain was raised during lean times. In some instances, bakers used the guild to exert pressure on town authorities to decrease prices of grain or lower standards of quality. In many regions, bakers were successful at securing a monopoly—thereby controlling their incomes to a degree—by limiting the amount of ovens in any town. Outside of town, most monasteries and castles had their own ovens, which were not regulated. Since people could not bake in their homes, many traveled to their bakery with a homemade loaf and had it baked for a fee.

This fourteenth-century illumination is a part of the manuscript titled The Grain Merchant. *Medieval businessmen sold wheat, oats, and barley, which were used during the Middle Ages to brew ale, or beer.*

Bakers sometimes offered other items in addition to standard loaves in a variety of weights and textures. The medieval version of "white" bread, for instance, which was made with refined flour, was the most expensive bread of the time. Most people consumed dark, rustic breads. Bakers often supplied fairs and markets with a version of gingerbread as well. This usually took the shape of small cakes or cookies that featured a guild seal or gingerbread men.

Bakers were generally male, though some women were employed to knead dough. Bakers generally hired two male apprentices, both of whom learned the craft within a few years. A baker was permitted to allow members of his family to work without pay, unlike most other trades.

Fresh ginger root appears above a traditionally shaped gingerbread man in these contemporary photographs. Because ginger helped preserve breads and cakes, it found its way into many medieval recipes.

Gingerbread Men*

For this project, you will make traditional gingerbread cookies similar to those found at fairs throughout much of medieval Europe. Although Europeans used honey to sweeten their baked goods, we will use sugar.
* ADULT SUPERVISION IS ADVISED FOR THIS CRAFT.

YOU WILL NEED
- Two large bowls
- Two small finger bowls
- Assorted utensils, measuring cups, and spoons
- Cookie sheet
- Parchment paper
- Toothpicks
- Protective oven mit

Recipe
1 cup granulated sugar
1½ tsp. baking soda
2½ cups all-purpose flour
¼ tsp. ground ginger
1 tsp. cinnamon

1 egg
½ cup molasses
½ cup solid vegetable shortening, softened

Step 1
In a large bowl, combine measured dry ingredients. Set aside.

Step 2
In another bowl, combine measured wet ingredients: egg, molasses, and softened vegetable shortening. Gradually add your dry ingredients to your wet ingredients and mix by hand. Work the mixture into a doughy consistency.

Step 3
After you are satisfied with your gingerbread dough, refrigerate it for about an hour. Next, line a cookie sheet with parchment paper and grease it lightly. Put a few tablespoons of flour in one small bowl and a few tablespoons of sugar in another. Set aside.

Step 4

Next, preheat oven to 350 degrees. Remove your dough from the refrigerator and sprinkle the dough's surface with flour. To shape your gingerbread men, make a series of six balls: Make one large ball for the gingerbread man's body and five smaller-sized balls for the arms, legs, and head. Gently shape them together and flatten them to look like typical gingerbread men. Sprinkle them with sugar. Try to size them equally so they cook evenly.

Step 5

Make impressions in your gingerbread men by poking a series of small holes in them with a toothpick. Poke two holes for eyes, make a curved line for a smile, and make three holes for buttons.

Step 6

Bake your cookies about 8 to 10 minutes at 350 degrees. They should be slightly browned around their edges. Remove from the pan with a spatula to cool. Your overall yield will depend on the size of your cookies.

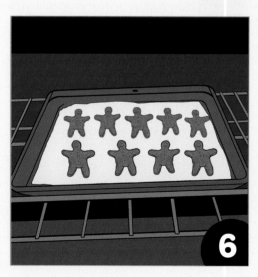

Weavers

The French monks in these fifteenth-century stained-glass panels are brushing and combing cloth. Weavers and cloth workers were among the largest group of artisans in medieval Europe.

The process of cloth making was incredibly industrialized in Europe during medieval times. By 1360, England was so skilled at producing excellent wool that it exported finished fabrics throughout Europe.

Like the stonemason's guild, the guilds of the textile industry had members who did a variety of jobs, some of which splintered off into new groups as they gained members. Various positions included wool dyers, fullers, combers, carders, spinners, and weavers. Skilled women who worked at home and were paid a set rate did much of this work. A master weaver-draper oversaw the production process, working with other laborers to create fabric from raw wool.

Once the wool was carded and combed, it was spun into yarn. When the yarn was ready for weaving, it was transported to a weaver's shop. Afterward, unfinished wools were washed in vats of hot water, stomped upon, and felted (reduced and matted) in a process called fulling. Then, the fulled cloth was processed again and made ready for transport, this time to the dyers. (Unfinished cloth was called "grey goods.") The finest woolen fabric of the period was called scarlet.

Dyes were tremendously expensive, purple being the costliest. Red dye,

Medieval tapestry makers sit below large framed tapestries in progress. While only the wealthy could commission master weavers to make tapestries to adorn castle walls, ordinary folks sometimes painted plain cloth to decorate and warm their homes.

made from the red, fleshy root of the madder plant, was also costly. It was usually reserved for nobility. Blue was the most common dye, made from the dried leaves of the woad plant. Yellow came from the stamens of crocus flowers. Dyeing was itself a complex process that involved the use of a mordant, a substance such as alum or vinegar, to make the dye stay on the wool.

Weavers worked alone or in pairs depending on the width of the fabric. Weaving was a skill that took years to master. (Tapestry weavers, for instance, often apprenticed for a period of no less than twelve years.) Sitting or standing at his or her loom, a weaver inserted a shuttle, a small piece of wood with a thread attached, over and under vertical warp threads. He or she then moved the shuttle, continuing the over-and-under pattern, across weft threads,

which were fixed horizontally. Once the cloth was woven, the yarns were compacted together and smoothed by brushing.

Although most outer garments were made of wool, including overcoats and tunics, people of nobility also enjoyed undergarments made from linen and silk.

An image of a peasant mowing oats is part of a fourteenth-century manuscript, by Aldebrando da Firenze, that details a variety of medical treatments.

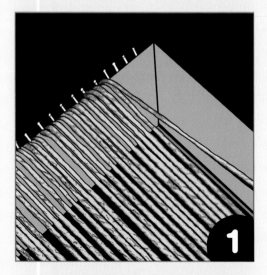

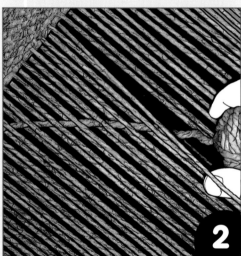

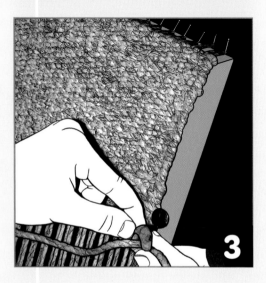

Peasant's Hat*

Practice basic weaving by making a rectangular cloth that can be sewn into a simple peasant's hat.
* ADULT SUPERVISION IS ADVISED FOR THIS CRAFT.

YOU WILL NEED
- Large wooden picture frame
- Nails
- Hammer
- 2 large skeins of wool yarn
- Scissors
- Thumbtacks
- Needle and thread

Step 1
To make a loom, hammer nails 1/2 inch apart along the top and bottom of your rectangular frame. Tie the end of your wool to the first nail and wrap the wool around the nails vertically, as shown.

Step 2
After the loom is strung, take a small ball of wool and tie the end to the first nail as well. Weave the yarn through alternate strands, pulling it gently from both sides as you weave to keep it as uniform as possible.

Step 3
When you have woven all the yarn in your first ball of wool, simply tie another length to the end of the first strand and continue weaving. Use thumbtacks to pin the sides of your weave to the loom to help keep straight the sides of the woven material. (Pulling the yarn tightly through the loom causes the weave to buckle. Don't worry if this happens; you can still use the finished piece, even if it's oddly shaped.)

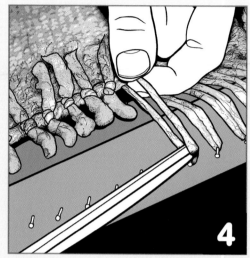

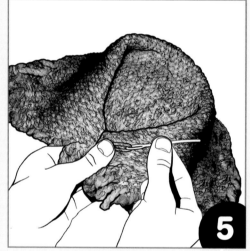

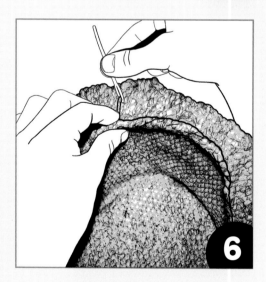

Step 4

When you have woven to about three inches from the bottom of the frame, tie the end in place. Cut the wool from the nails along the bottom and tie each one in a knot, as shown. Once removed from the loom, do the same to the top loops.

Step 5

To make a simple peasant hat from your woven mat, take two corners and fold them together, as shown. Sew them in place with a needle and thread.

Step 6

Pinch a band along the inside of the hat and sew a line, as shown. Roll the outer edge into a rim and sew it in place.

31

Armorers

P late armor, among the most useful items in a knight's possession, was incredibly time-consuming to make and expensive to buy. Even to this day, plate armor is recognized as one of the most advanced inventions of the medieval period. It is considered remarkable because of the difficulty an armorer would have had in crafting the material.

First, the manufacture of plate armor required a number of natural resources, including power from a waterwheel, iron ore, charcoal, and a variety of highly skilled workers who knew how to forge and smelt metal. Because of the need for abundant wood (to make charcoal) and iron ore, only two regions in Europe became well known for plate armor production: northern Italy and southern Germany.

The armorer would have needed a pure type of iron to create plate armor. This iron was processed in iron mines.

In this illustration, medieval blacksmiths are at work heating iron by intensifying the fires with large bellows and then hammering the heated iron into shape. Making armor was a distinct and highly desirable skill during the Middle Ages, and only a few areas of Europe became know for its production.

The iron was broken down and heated to produce iron blooms, an impure form of melted iron. The blooms were then reheated and hammered to force out the impurities. Once prepared and made as pure as possible, these iron pieces were transported by pack animals to the armorer.

Armorers used a process called forging to create plate armor. Unlike what most people imagine, armorers did not want the plate to be of equal thickness because it would have been too weak. The best plate armor was made thinner

The sword and scabbard (sword covering) in this image belonged to a member of the Holy Roman army. Blacksmiths understood how to fashion metals into useful and effective swords from the beginning of the Middle Ages.

around the edges where it was joined. Most armorers were so experienced that they could hammer the hot metal by hand, estimating by sight whether its thickness was appropriate. Charcoal heated the metal and gradually released carbon, which transferred to the iron and made it stronger while it was being forged. After cutting the sheets of iron, groups of men would beat the heated iron into rough plates to shape each piece. This process was repeated until the desired shape was obtained. Medieval armorers were probably not aware of the chemical process that was taking place when the carbon transferred to the iron created steel. Instead, armorers were aware of the colors the metal had to achieve in order to make it suitable for withstanding battle. This was most likely among the secrets of the armorers' trade.

As the individual plates were completed, they were assembled and tested for size and then taken apart again. The last step involved using the waterwheel to power grinding stones that smoothed each piece. This process removed the hammer marks and polished the metal to a brilliant shine.

This suit of fifteenth-century plate armor was made in medieval France. Plate armor was difficult and time-consuming to produce and expensive to buy. It was among the most challenging gear to obtain for young medieval knights.

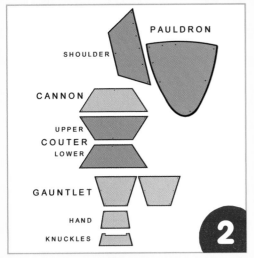

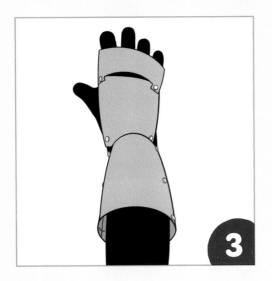

Armor

For this project you can use a variety of recycled aluminum containers to create plate armor that resembles what a knight would have worn in battle. Armor can be made for both arms by repeating steps 1–6.

* ADULT SUPERVISION IS REQUIRED FOR THIS CRAFT.

YOU WILL NEED

- Aluminum baking pans/lids
- Paper fasteners
- 1 yd. of black felt
- Needle and thread or sewing machine
- Scissors
- Awl
- Construction paper
- Masking tape
- Pencil
- Tape
- Protective gloves

Step 1

Trace your hand and arm, all the way up to your shoulder, on a large piece of construction paper or two shorter pieces joined by tape on the reverse sides. Spread your fingers apart when tracing your hand. Cut out the pattern leaving a 1/2-inch border all around. Trace the pattern twice onto felt, one for the front of your arm and one for the back. Sew these two sleeves together to make one long glove.

Step 2

Before making your armor out of metal, begin with a paper pattern. Use the simple shapes, shown here, and roughly proportion them to the size of your glove (arm).

Step 3

Use paper fasteners to attach the paper hand pattern to the knuckle plate pattern. Join the two gauntlet side patterns together with fasteners making a cone shape.

Step 4

Take the lower couter pattern and join its pointed ends together with a paper fastener. Do the same with the

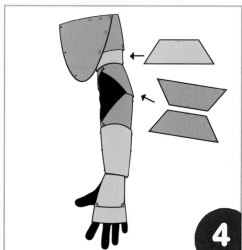

upper couter pattern. Fit these around the glove's elbow area. Attach the cannon pattern in the same way at the biceps. Cut the pauldron pattern to fit over your chest and shoulders.

Step 5

Now that your pattern is cut, take all of the shapes apart to trace them onto large aluminum baking sheets with a pencil. Wearing protective gloves, cut out the pieces with scissors and assemble them using the same methods as you did with the paper patterns. Use an awl to make holes into the felt to hold the armor to it with paper fasteners.

Step 6

Fold the top point of the pauldron over, making a cone shape at the top. This cone rests on your shoulder. Attach the top of the felt sleeve over the short sleeves of a black T-shirt, using safety pins.

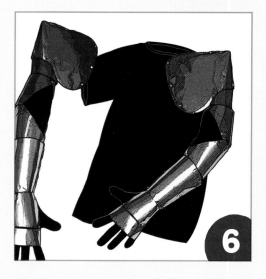

Shoemakers

Shoemakers displayed their wares from small shop windows overlooking the street, just like other medieval artisans of the day. At the time, shoemakers were called cordwainers, after the finest and most expensive leather of their trade, which was imported from the Muslim city of Córdoba in Spain.

Cordovan leather was among the softest and most flexible leather available, and it was the easiest leather to sew. It came from Musoli goatskin—a species of goat found only throughout the Iberian Peninsula—and was softened in a special, secret process known only to the Muslims there. This method used alum, a mordant common in the fabric trades. Cordovan leather was brought to the rest of western Europe during the period of the Crusades. At that time, European knights discovered shoes made with the softest leather they had ever felt when fighting to reestablish Christianity in Spain.

Most European shoemakers used less expensive grades of leather, such as

Leather was used for a variety of items in medieval Europe, including shoes, manuscript pages, and bindings. It was also used to cover glass containers to keep them from breaking. In this anonymous fifteenth-century manuscript, a man is stretching animal skin for one such purpose.

sheepskin and cowhide. These animal skins were toughened in a process called tanning, which made the material more resilient to weather and wear. The tanneries where leather was prepared, like the places where wool was dyed, smelled awful from chemicals and dyes. Because of this, most townspeople insisted that tanneries remain on the outskirts of town.

Most medieval shoes were like moccasins since they had no arch supports or heels. Most had rounded fronts during the early Middle Ages, but styles later became more pointed, which was considered fashionable. Much of the information we have about shoe styles of the era has come from shoes depicted in artwork of the period, as most medieval leather goods have since rotted away. Archaeologists have found priceless examples of medieval leather shoes and boots intact, however. These discoveries were made in archaeological digs along the banks of the Thames River in London, into which people for years threw their garbage and worn items. Most shoes had drawstrings and laces. Some had miniature loops where laces were strung, and others simply wrapped around the entire boot. Centuries later, when styles became more pointed, shoes often had buckles or toggles to secure them to feet. Some were dyed green, red, black, or cream. Others were embroidered or had designs pressed into the leather, though these shoes would have been intended only for use indoors.

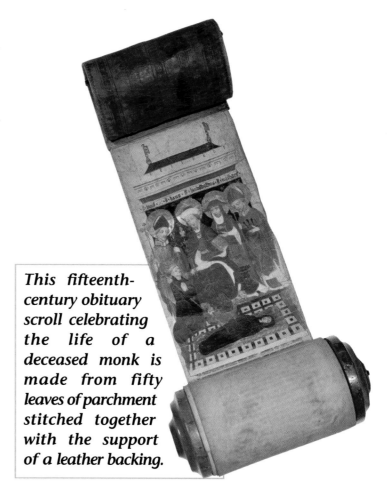

This fifteenth-century obituary scroll celebrating the life of a deceased monk is made from fifty leaves of parchment stitched together with the support of a leather backing.

In addition to shoes, tanned leather was sold to craftsmen who made a variety of other items, including gloves, belts, small bags, and purses. Even some glass bottles were covered in leather since glass was rare and quite fragile.

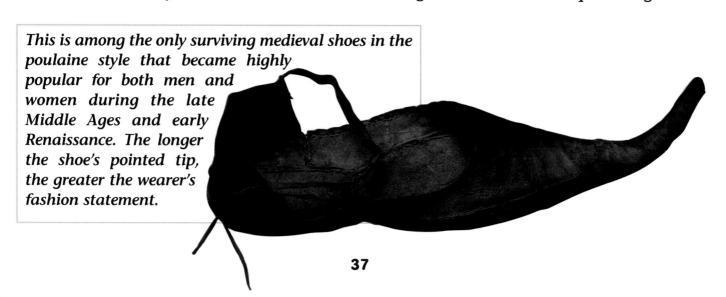

This is among the only surviving medieval shoes in the poulaine style that became highly popular for both men and women during the late Middle Ages and early Renaissance. The longer the shoe's pointed tip, the greater the wearer's fashion statement.

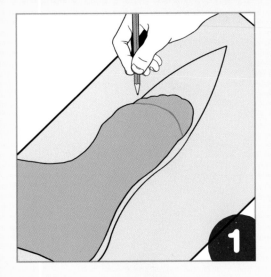

Shoes*

You have been commissioned to sew a pair of pointed poulaine shoes for the head of the weavers' guild, but your shoes will be made out of felt, not leather.
* ADULT SUPERVISION IS ADVISED FOR THIS CRAFT.

YOU WILL NEED
- **Brown craft foam sheet**
- **1 yd. of brown felt**
- **Needle and brown thread**
- **Scissors**
- **Construction paper**
- **Pencil**

Step 1
Trace your foot onto a piece of construction paper. Add a long point to extend from the toes, as shown.

Step 2
Cut the paper pattern out. Trace and cut one of these patterns from your craft foam sheet, and then turn the pattern over and trace and cut another for your opposite foot. These will be the soles of your shoes.

Step 3
Place your foot onto the sole and cut a triangle out of felt that fits around the front instep of your foot. Use the first one as a pattern for the second shoe. Sew both to the soles as shown.

Step 4
Cut a rectangular band of felt that wraps around the heel/ankle of the sole to the ends of the front piece. Cut another rectangular band, exactly the same size, for the second shoe. Sew each along the sole of each shoe.

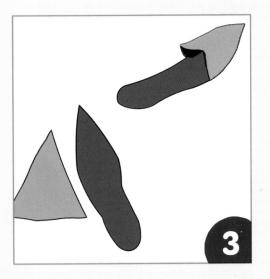

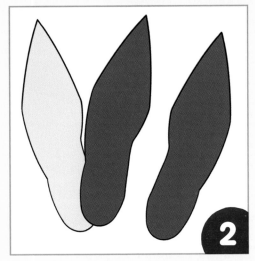

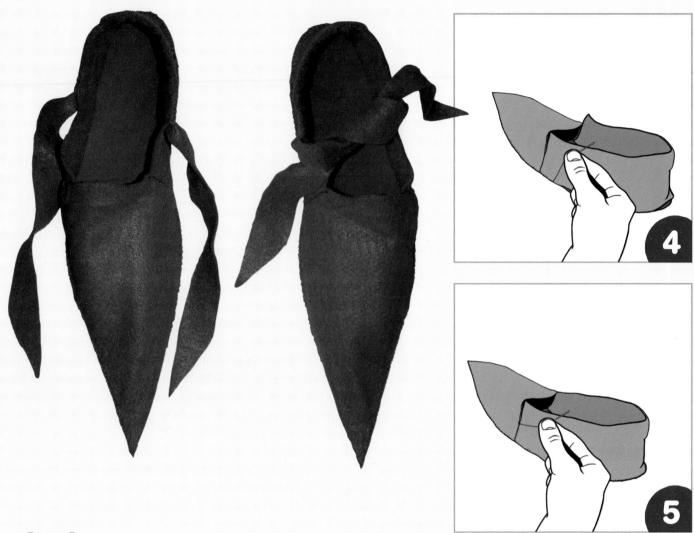

Step 5

Stitch the two pieces (the triangles from step 3 and the rectangles from step 4) from the base of the soles where they meet to the instep on both sides of each shoe.

Step 6

Cut two long felt bands each about eight to ten inches in length depending on your shoe size. These bands should wrap around your ankle and extend to the tip of your shoe. They will be your shoe's ties. Sew them to the backs of your shoes around the ankle.

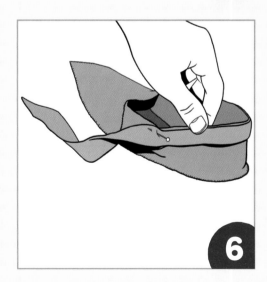

Potters

ISTAVRATO LANNO 1729 SOTTo
° GREG° BIASSI CASTALDO.

°V RESTAVRATO SOTO M° Z GIACOMO RIZZO ET CONPAGNI. 1630.

Master potters can be seen in this fifteenth-century Italian painting, Sign of the Guild of the Potters. *Pottery guilds were somewhat less influential than other guilds in medieval Italy.*

During the Middle Ages, many potters started out as peasants who dug in the earth for natural clays, kneaded them, and worked them on a potter's wheel. These techniques did not change much throughout the period. Finished pieces were used as jugs, jars, dishes, bowls, and pitchers. Many were plain, though some were decorated during the later part of the Middle Ages. Some even had animals or human forms. "Face" jugs—vessels that featured a human face—were quite exquisite and unusual. Many times, pottery was available for those people who could not afford the same items in bronze, silver, or gold.

In the early years, peasants needed few materials to turn out beautiful and useful items made of clay. As long as a supply of clay, sand, and wood was available, peasants were able to make kilns where the clay was fired in a process that made it hard and waterproof. Chances are that families passed these skills down from generation to generation. When potters finally made their way into medieval towns in the twelfth and thirteenth centuries, theirs was considered among the least influential of guilds. Even so, master potters had to construct pieces by hand (using the coil, pinch, or slab methods)

and be able to accurately "throw" them on the potter's wheel, which was driven by foot.

The best pottery came from Italy, Spain, and Germany, which was famous for it clay beer mugs. (Most people drank beverages from wooden containers.) The beautifully decorated pottery that originated on the Spanish island of Majorca often featured elaborate designs in animal, bird, and leaf patterns. Italians, who had been trading (and fighting) with the Spanish Muslims, saw this exquisite pottery and were inspired to create similarly styled items. The Italian city of Florence became known for this decorated pottery, which was called *majolica*, named after the Spanish island where it originated.

These earthenware jugs featuring animal designs in their painted glazes were highly sought after by medieval nobility. The jugs were imported from Spain for serving wine and ale. The style was later adopted by the Italians.

Clay Jug

Try your hand as a potter by making this essential piece of table-ware, a ceramic jug with a human face.

YOU WILL NEED
- Air-hardening clay
- Clay knife/tools
- Paints/paintbrushes
- A small bowl filled with water for "slip"
- Sponge
- Gloss or satin medium

Step 1

Begin by preparing your work surface. Knead the clay so it's more pliable and has fewer air bubbles. Fill a small bowl with cold water and add a quarter teaspoon-sized amount of clay to the water. As it dissolves, it will create "slip," a bonding agent that joins pieces of clay. Next, roll a large ball from clay. Press your fingers into its top to slightly hollow it out. Roll another piece of clay into a long coil, like an earthworm. Attach the ends together to form a band. Score the clay with a clay knife and use slip to attach it to the bottom of the ball as a base.

Step 2

To make the neck of the jug, form a rectangle out of clay and smooth its surface. Attach it to the top of the ball by using the score and slip method from step 1. The lip of the jug takes the shape of a tiny shield. Again, use the scoring and slip method to attach the lip to the left side of the jug. Gently sculpt it so that it is in proportion to the rest of the jug.

Step 3

To make the handle, make a long rectangle, roughly four or five inches in length and no more than an inch wide. Attach the handle by using the score and slip

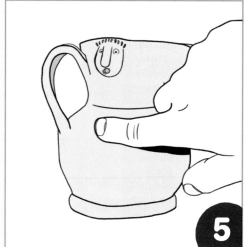

method. Smooth out the areas where you have joined the pieces with your fingers.

Step 4
Next, use a small bit of clay to add the human head. Poke holes with a toothpick for eyes, mouth, etc.

Step 5
Smooth the surface of the entire jug until you are satisfied with your sculpture. Set it aside to dry overnight.

Step 6
Once your jug is completely dry, you can mix some watered-down craft paint to add the animal designs and features for the human head. After the paint dries, cover it with a layer of gloss or satin medium to make it shiny.

TIMELINE

AD `313` Constantine imposes the Edict of Milan, preaching tolerance for Christianity.

`410` Visigoths sack Rome.

`circa 476` The Roman Empire falls.

`476–1000` The period historians sometimes refer to as Europe's Dark Ages.

`circa 700` Feudal system is established in France.

`711` Muslims invade Spain.

`768` Charlemagne becomes king of the Franks.

`793` Beginning of Viking raids in England.

`1066` William the Conqueror conquers England.

`1095` Pope Urban II urges Christian knights to defend Christianity.

`1096–1291` The Christian Crusades are launched to recapture the Holy Land from Muslims.

`1161` First guilds are established; the era of cathedral-building begins.

`1171` The Bank of Venice opens.

`1179` The third Lateran Council decrees all cathedrals must have schools.

`1180` Windmills first appear in Europe.

`1215` The fourth Lateran Council requires Jews to wear identifying badges; signing of the Magna Carta.

`1241` Mongols invade Europe.

`1271` Marco Polo travels to Asia.

`1300` Feudalism ends.

`1314–1322` The great famine (alternate droughts and heavy rains in northern Europe).

`1337–1453` Hundred Years' War between England and France.

`1347–1530` The plague kills about 25 million people throughout Europe.

`1381` Peasants' Revolt.

`1453` The fall of Constantinople to Ottoman Turks (often taken as end of the Middle Ages).

GLOSSARY

apprentice A young person who studied under a master artisan during the Middle Ages in order to learn a specific craft.

charter A written agreement or contract that outlined a town's area, its privileges to collect tolls and taxes, and its authority to begin an independent system of government.

Crusades A series of religious wars fought between Christians and Muslims that occurred during the Middle Ages between 1096 and 1291.

fair A large market in a specific city for a fixed period of time where goods were sold and traded.

full To increase the weight of fabric by applying pressure to condense its threads and heat to shrink it.

Hanseatic League A trading alliance of German "Hanse" towns along the Baltic Sea that had a monopoly of regional trade in northern Europe.

journeyman In the Middle Ages, a skilled craftsman who had risen in status from that of an apprentice and who often traveled with goods to sell or trade with others.

lord A male knight and/or noble who was given land by the king and who lived at a large estate or castle.

master An artisan who was a member of a guild and was expertly skilled in a specific craft.

masterpiece The finished craft a journeyman had to complete in order to be admitted into a guild.

Middle Ages A period of time in western Europe between the fall of the Roman Empire in AD 476 and the beginning of the Renaissance in the fifteenth century.

secular Nonreligious.

serf A peasant laborer who was bound to his lord to work the land where he was born and perform duties for the lord.

warp In weaving, the vertical lengths of yarn or thread that are crossed by the horizontal weft threads.

weft In weaving, the horizontal threads that are laced through the warp threads.

FOR MORE INFORMATION

The Metropolitan Museum of Art
1000 Fifth Avenue
New York, NY 10028-0198
(212) 535-7710
Web site: http://www.metmuseum.org

The Pierpont Morgan Library
29 East 36th Street
New York, NY 10016
(212) 685-0610
Web site: http://www.morganlibrary.org

Web Sites

Due to the changing nature of Internet links, the Rosen Publishing Group, Inc., has developed an online list of Web sites related to the subject of this book. This site is updated regularly. Please use the link below to access the list:

http://www.rosenlinks.com/ccma/megu

FOR FURTHER READING

Bishop, Morris. *The Middle Ages*. Boston, MA: Houghton Mifflin Company, 1987.

Chrisp, Peter. *Town and Country Life* (Medieval Realms). San Diego, CA: Lucent Publishers, 2004.

Corbishley, Mike. *The Middle Ages* (Cultural Atlas for Young People). New York, NY: Facts on File, 2003.

Gies, Joseph, and Frances Gies. *Life in a Medieval City*. New York, NY: Harper & Row, 1981.

Newman, Paul, B. *Daily Life in the Middle Ages*. Jefferson, NC: McFarland & Co., Inc., 2001.

Rowling, Marjorie. *Life in Medieval Times*. New York, NY: Penguin Putnam, 1973.

INDEX

ABOUT THE AUTHOR/ILLUSTRATOR

Joann Jovinelly and Jason Netelkos have collaborated on many educational projects for young people. This is their second crafts series encouraging youngsters to learn history through hands-on projects. Their first series, Crafts of the Ancient World, was published by the Rosen Publishing Group in 2001. They live in New York City.

PHOTO CREDITS